Wonders

Mc
Graw
Hill
Education

Cover: Nathan Love

mheducation.com/prek-12

Send all inquiries to:
McGraw-Hill Education
Two Penn Plaza
New York, New York 10121

ISBN: 978-0-07-906633-6
MHID: 0-07-906633-X

Printed in the United States of America.

2 3 4 5 6 7 8 9 QVS 23 22 21 20 19

B

Program Authors

Diane August

Donald R. Bear

Kathy R. Bumgardner

Jana Echevarria

Douglas Fisher

David J. Francis

Vicki Gibson

Jan Hasbrouck

Timothy Shanahan

Josefina V. Tinajero

Mc Graw Hill Education

UNIT

3

Changes Over Time

SOCIAL STUDIES

WEEK I WHAT TIME IS IT?

On My Way to School Fantasy 6
by Wong Herbert Yee

Read Together **It's About Time** Nonfiction 24

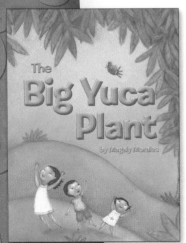

SCIENCE

WEEK 2 WATCH IT GROW!

The Big Yuca Plant Drama 28
by Magaly Morales

Read Together **How Plants Grow** Nonfiction 46

my.mheducation.com

WEEK 3 TALES OVER TIME

The Gingerbread Man Folktale. 50
by Wiley Blevins; illustrated by Richard Egielski

 Mother Goose Rhymes Poetry 68

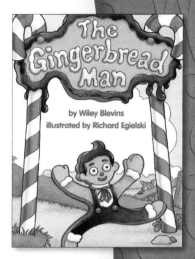

WEEK 4 NOW AND THEN

Long Ago and Now Nonfiction 74
by Minda Novek

 From Horse to Plane Nonfiction. . . . 90

WEEK 5 FROM FARM TO TABLE

From Cows to You Nonfiction. 94

 A Food Chart Nonfiction 102

Glossary 104

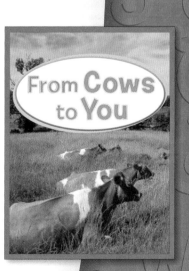

Genre Fantasy

Essential Question

How do we measure time?

Read about the funny things that make a boy late for school.

Go Digital!

6

On My Way to School

by Wong Herbert Yee

On my **way** to school **today**,
a pig asks me to come and play.

It's not just a pig.
It's a pig in a wig!
We run for the bus,
just the two of us.

Pig and I run fast, fast, fast!
We get on the bus at last.
Huff, puff! The bus zips **away**.
Pig makes me late for school today!

On my way to school, we pass
a trash truck that ran out of gas.
On top of that truck,
sit two apes and a duck!

Apes and a duck hop in the bus.
They sit down with the rest of us.

Slip, flip! The bus zips away.
Apes make me late for school today!

On my way to school, I see
some frogs in a gumdrop tree.

Plip, plop! The gumdrops drop.
Two frogs cut. Two frogs mop.

Frogs hop in the bus.

They sit down with the rest of us.

Hip! Hop! The bus zips away.

Frogs make me late for school today!

Here we go, just one last stop.
Frogs hop in the lake. Plip, plop!

Duck is off to get some gas.
Apes fish and nap in the grass.

Tick, tock! The bus zips away.
It looks like I am late today!

Now the bus drops me off at school.
I see a crocodile slink out of a pool!

20

I think it slid under the gate.
And that, Miss Blake, is **why** I am late!

Meet Wong Herbert Yee

Wong Herbert Yee says, "No bus picked me up at the corner. I walked a mile to get to school! When I write, I use things that really happened. My imagination fills in the rest. Remember what you see, read, and hear. You may write a funny story, too!"

Author's Purpose

Wong Herbert Yee wanted to write a funny story about getting to school. Draw how you get to school. Write about it.

Judy Yee

Respond to the Text

Retell

Use your own words to retell *On My Way to School.*

Beginning
↓
Middle
↓
End

Write

Write 4 more pages of the story. Tell the excuses the boy might give his mom for getting home late. Try these sentence starters:

When the bell rang...
Next, I saw a...

Make Connections

COLLABORATE

How is time important in this story?

ESSENTIAL QUESTION

23

Compare Texts

Read about ways we can tell the time.

It's About Time!

Beep, beep, beep!
An alarm **clock** wakes you up.
It's time for school!

How do you know what time it is?
The numbers on a clock tell you.

Some clocks have faces with hands.
The hands point to the numbers.
Some clocks have just numbers.

All clocks tell the **hour** and **minute**.
There are 60 minutes in an hour.
There are 60 **seconds** in a minute.

(t) McGraw-Hill Education; (b) Stockbyte/EyeWire/Getty Images

Long ago, people didn't have clocks.
They used the sun to tell time instead.

Tools like **sundials** helped them.
The sun's **shadow** showed the hour.
But people had to guess the minutes.
What time is this sundial showing?

Then people made clocks! It was easy to see the hour and minutes. There were big clocks and little clocks.

Today watches, phones, and computers tell the time, too. We always know the time!

Make Connections

 What might help the boy in *On My Way to School* get to school on time? **Essential Question**

Genre Drama

Essential Question
How do plants change as they grow?

Read about a girl whose plant grows too much.

Go Digital!

The Big Yuca Plant

by Magaly Morales

Meet the Characters

Narrator

Paco

Lola

Ana

Dad

Mom

Pig

Cat

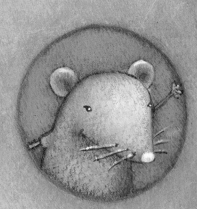

Rat

	Narrator	A girl is planting.
	Paco	Hello, Sis. What plant is that?
	Lola	It is a yuca. It should **grow** a root that we can eat.
	Paco	Yum! Can we help you?

31

 Lola   Yes. Ana can help me dig.
You can get the plant **water**.

 Paco   The sun will shine and the
plant will grow.

 Ana   Grow, plant, grow!

Narrator	Many days pass.
Dad	Look at the size of that plant.
Mom	Yes, it is **green** and **pretty**. But it is as big as we are!

Lola	My yuca did grow! It is time to pull it up.
Narrator	She tugs and tugs.
Lola	I can't get it. It is too big!
Paco	I will help. I will grab you. You grab the plant.

 Lola   This plant is stuck!

 Ana   I can tug. Come up, yuca!

 Dad   That is quite a plant!
                                 Let us help.

 Narrator Mom and Dad tug. But the
                                 plant does not come up.

Paco There are five of us pulling.
But the yuca is still stuck.

Lola Who can we ask for help?

Mom Ask Pig. Pig is big. She can tug.

Lola Pig, can you help?

Pig Yes, I will help. I will tug Mom.

 Mom And I will tug Dad.

 Dad And I will tug Ana.

 Ana And I will tug Paco.

 Paco And I will tug Lola.

 Lola And I will tug the yuca plant.

 Narrator But the plant does not move a bit.

 Ana This plant can't be picked.

 Lola Yes, it can! There must be a way. We can ask Cat.

 Paco Cat, will you help?

 Cat   But I am not big like Pig.

 Lola   You can still help. **Together** we can get the yuca out.

 Cat   I will do my best.

	Narrator	They all tug. But the plant is still stuck.
	Lola	**Should** we ask that rat to help?
	Paco	A rat? A rat is little. He can't help.
	Rat	Yes, I can.

 Rat Take this vine. Tie it to the plant. We all must tug on the vine.

 Lola Yes, do as Rat said!

 Narrator They get in a line.

 Lola Grab the vine and tug!

Dad	It is out at last!
Ana	What a fine yuca.
Pig	It could win a prize.

42

Mom We all must thank Rat.

Lola You are little, but you are wise.

All Thank you!

About Magaly Morales

Magaly Morales says, "In my family, we are very close. We all help each other. When I need something, I know I can count on my family, just as Lola counts on hers. Together we are stronger and smarter than when we are by ourselves."

Magaly Morales

Author's Purpose

Magaly Morales likes to draw people helping each other. Draw yourself helping a friend or someone in your family. Write about your picture.

Respond to the Text

Retell

Use your own words to retell *The Big Yuca Plant*. Tell what happens in order.

First
↓
Next
↓
Then
↓
Last

Write

What else might Rat say? Write some more lines for Rat at the end of the play. Use these sentence starters:

> Rat is small but...
> Rat wanted to...

Make Connections
COLLABORATE

? How is Lola's yuca like a plant you have seen?

ESSENTIAL QUESTION

Compare Texts

Read about how plants grow and change.

How Plants Grow

These are all seeds.

A plant's life begins as a **seed**. Inside the seed is a little, new plant.

When the seed is planted, a **root** grows down in the soil. The root holds the seed in the soil. It takes in water, too.

The stem grows up from the seed. When it pops out of the soil, it is called a **sprout**. Green leaves grow on the stem.

The leaves have a big job. They make food for the plant to live. The leaves use water, sunlight, and air to make food.

blossom

fruit

Over time, blossoms pop up on the plant. These blossoms are the plant's flowers. They can grow into a fruit such as this pumpkin. Many fruits can grow on one plant vine.

Inside the fruit are seeds. These seeds can be used to grow new plants.

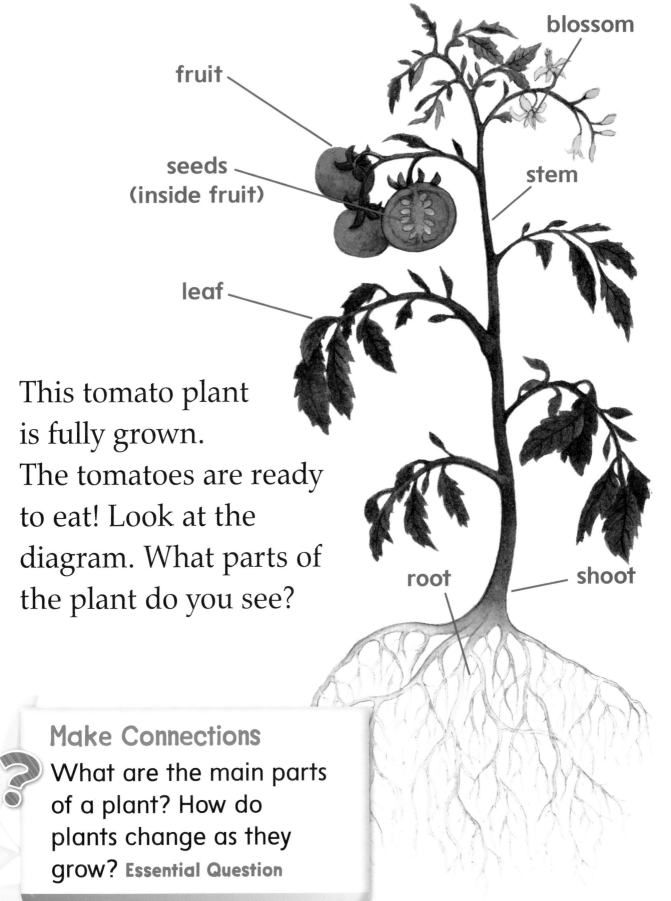

fruit

seeds
(inside fruit)

leaf

blossom

stem

root

shoot

This tomato plant
is fully grown.
The tomatoes are ready
to eat! Look at the
diagram. What parts of
the plant do you see?

Make Connections

? What are the main parts
of a plant? How do
plants change as they
grow? **Essential Question**

Essential Question

What is a folktale?

Read a classic tale about a man who is made out of gingerbread.

Go Digital!

50

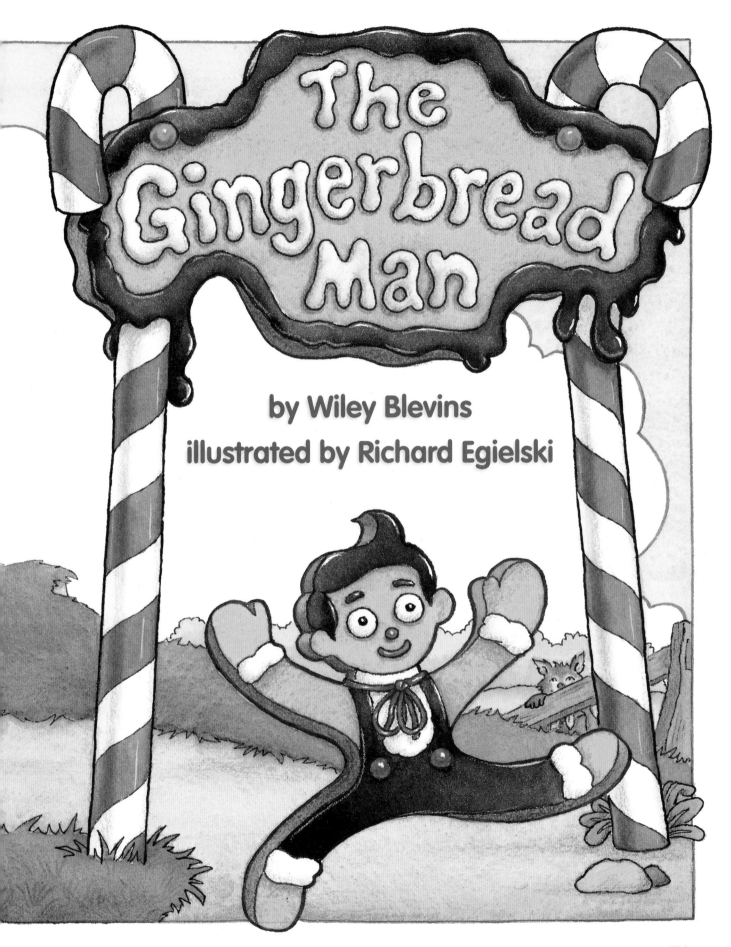

The Gingerbread Man

by Wiley Blevins

illustrated by Richard Egielski

Once upon a time there lived a little Gram and a little Gramps. They had a **happy** life. Except for one big thing. They did not have **any** grandkids.

"I will make a grandson out of gingerbread," said Gram.

"That will be nice," said Gramps.

So Gram made a little gingerbread man. Then she placed him in the oven to bake.

At last, it was time to take him out.
Gram set him down. She gave him a
happy face. She gave him pants made
of fudge icing.

Just as she finished, the Gingerbread
Man jumped up. Like magic! He
looked at Gram and Gramps and
smiled. Then he ran away.

Gram and Gramps raced after him.

"Run, run, run as fast as you can. You can't catch me. I'm the Gingerbread Man," the little man sang.

Gram and Gramps did not catch him.

The Gingerbread Man ran on and on. He ran until he met a black cow.

"Stop!" yelled the black cow. "You smell good. I will eat you up. Yum!"

"I ran **from** Gram and Gramps," the Gingerbread Man sang. "I can run from you, too. Yes, I can, can, can!"

The Gingerbread Man ran and ran.
And the cow did not catch him.

Next, the Gingerbread Man met a
white duck.

"Do not run so fast," said the duck.
"I am hungry. You will make a nice
snack. Yum, yum!"

"I ran from the cow and Gram and Gramps," yelled the Gingerbread Man. "And I can run from you, too. Yes, I can, can, can!"

And the duck did not catch him.

The Gingerbread Man ran on and on and on. He passed a red fox.

"Run, run, run just as fast as you can. You can't catch me. I'm the Gingerbread Man," he sang.

"I do not wish to catch you," said the fox. "I just wish to be a friend."

The Gingerbread Man and the fox ran on until they came to the edge of a big lake.

"But I can't swim," said the Gingerbread Man. "What will I do?"

"Jump on my back," said the red fox.
"I will help."

So, the Gingerbread Man jumped on
top of the red fox. The red fox swam
and swam and swam.

"Oh, no," said the red fox. "My back is sinking. Jump on my head. Quick! If not, you will get wet."

The Gingerbread Man jumped on the fox's head. The fox tossed the Gingerbread Man up in the air.

"Oh, no!" yelled the Gingerbread Man. And then the fox ate him up.

"Run, run, run as fast as you can," said the fox. "This is the last of that Gingerbread Man."

Meet the Illustrator

Richard Egielski has enjoyed drawing since he was a boy. Now he loves to draw pictures for stories he writes and stories that other people write. He likes to illustrate stories about real people as well as make-believe characters.

Richard Egielski

Illustrator's Purpose

Richard Egielski wanted to illustrate a story about make-believe characters. Draw a favorite make-believe character from a folktale. Write what the character is doing.

Respond to the Text

Retell

Use your own words to retell *The Gingerbread Man*.

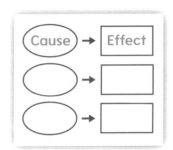

Write

Imagine that the Gingerbread Man decided to run around the lake. Then write a new ending to the story. Use these sentence frames:

The Gingerbread Man said...
Then the Gingerbread Man...

Make Connections

How is *The Gingerbread Man* like another folktale you know?

ESSENTIAL QUESTION

Compare Texts

Read some favorite rhymes from long ago.

Go Digital!

Mother Goose Rhymes

Children have been enjoying Mother Goose rhymes for a very long time. Your grandparents and their grandparents might have enjoyed the same rhymes that you enjoy today!

Illustration: Tomek Bogacki

Hickory, Dickory, Dock

Hickory, dickory, dock,
The mouse ran up the clock;
The clock struck one,
The mouse ran down;
Hickory, dickory, dock!

Higglety, Pigglety, Pop!

Higglety, pigglety, pop!
The dog has eaten the mop.
The pig's in a hurry.
The cat's in a flurry.
Higglety, pigglety, pop!

Hey! Diddle, Diddle

Hey! diddle, diddle,
The cat and the fiddle,
The cow jumped over the moon;
The little dog laughed
To see such sport,
And the dish ran away with the spoon.

Star Light

Star light, star bright,
First star I see tonight,
I wish I may, I wish I might
Have the wish I wish tonight.

Make Connections

How is a nursery rhyme like a folktale?

Essential Question

Essential Question

How is life different than it was long ago?

Read about now and long ago.

Go Digital!

Long Ago and Now

by Minda Novek

What was life like long **ago**?
In some ways it was the same as
today. But in many ways it was not.

Today, we ride in a car. It is a fast
way to go. It is fun to take a trip
with Mom and Dad.

Long ago, **people** rode in wagons.
It could take a long time to get
places.

These days, we have many things to help us at home. This is **how** food is kept fresh. This **boy** can get a snack at any time.

In **old** times, people kept things cold in a box filled with ice. Men drove trucks filled with ice to people's homes. This man uses tongs to lift a block of ice.

Today we can get water at home. This **girl** can clean up and take a drink at a sink.

Long ago, people used to get water at a pump. This boy pumps water into his bucket. Then, he has to carry the water all the way home!

These days, we have machines that help us. This is how we get clothes clean. This boy likes to help.

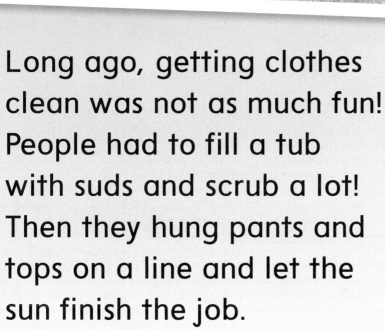

Long ago, getting clothes clean was not as much fun! People had to fill a tub with suds and scrub a lot! Then they hung pants and tops on a line and let the sun finish the job.

83

What do kids today have in common with kids long ago?

Back then, kids went to school just like us. Kids used pencils and paper. They read books in class and used books to look things up.

Today, we still use pencils, paper, and books at school. But there are new things we use in class, too. We can use computers to type. We use the Internet to look things up.

Ariel Skelley/Blend Images/Getty Images

Kids have always liked to play.
Some games have not changed
since long ago.

Back then, kids liked baseball and
circle games and skating.

Kids still like these old-time games today. Which one do you like best?

About Minda Novek

When **Minda Novek** was a little girl, she was already interested in how people lived long ago. She also likes to write about kids today who live in different lands. Minda uses photos for all these projects, so you can learn about real people.

Author's Purpose

Minda Novek wanted to compare life long ago with life today. Draw a picture of something long ago and a picture of something today. Write about each picture.

Respond to the Text

Retell

Use your own words to retell *Long Ago and Now*.

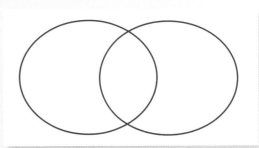

Write

Based on *Long Ago and Now*, do you think being a kid is better now, or was it better in the past? Why? Use these sentence starters:

Now, kids can...
Long ago, kids could...

Make Connections

What would it be like to go to a one-room school house?

ESSENTIAL QUESTION

Compare Texts

Read about how transportation has changed.

From Horse to Plane

People today can go places in cars, planes, and trains. Long ago there were not as many kinds of **transportation**. Before **engines**, people had to walk or use horses.

People rode in wagons pulled by horses.

(bkgd) Design Pics/Don Hammond; (b) Dynamic Graphics/Fotosearch

Trains go on rails to and from stations.

Then the train was **invented**. Steam engines made them go. Now people could go places much faster. It used to take days to go a hundred miles. After the train was invented, it might take hours.

Corbis

Years later, cars were invented. The first cars did not go very fast. Cars today can go faster. People like to ride in cars. They can go where they want.

The first cars were only a little faster than horses.

The first airplanes could not go far.

Soon, there was a faster way to go. The airplane was invented. Airplanes can go over mountains and oceans. Today we can go across the world in a day. That could take years long ago!

Make Connections

What transportation do you use? How is it different from long ago?

Essential Question

(bkg and tr) U.S. Air Force; (tl) Bettmann/Getty Images

Essential Question

How do we get our food?

Read about how we get milk.

Go Digital!

From Cows to You

Look at these dairy cows. They make the milk we drink. In spring and summer, these cows graze on green grass.

In winter, the cows move into the warm barn. The farmer gives them hay to eat. If cows eat good food, they make good milk.

Being a dairy farmer is hard **work**.
Cows must be milked **every** morning
and every evening.

On small farms,
farmers milk the
cows by hand.

On big farms,
farmers use milking
machines.

The milk goes into a big tank. The tank keeps the milk cold. Cold milk will not spoil. **Soon**, a milk truck takes the cow's milk to a dairy.

At the dairy, the milk is cooked. Bringing it to a boil will kill bad germs. Then, it is quickly cooled.

When that's **done**, machines put all the milk into cartons or jugs.

After that, cartons and jugs full of milk get sent to stores. They are put in the dairy case. Look at all the kinds of milk we can **buy**.

Who will drink the milk? You!

Milk is made into other foods.
Some dairy foods make our
bodies strong and healthy.
Thank you, cows!

Milk is cooked with
other things to make
cheese.

Butter comes from milk.

Milk is heated and
treated to make yogurt.

Fun Facts

Moooo!

- Most cows give enough milk every day to fill 90 glasses.

- Some farmers say that cows give more milk when there's music playing.

Respond to the Text

1. Use details from the selection to summarize. SUMMARIZE

2. Based on *From Cows to You,* which job in the milk process would you rather have? Why? WRITE

? 3. What other foods do we get from a farm? TEXT TO WORLD

Compare Texts

Learn how to use a food chart.

Read Together

A Food Chart

Dairy is one food group. The other food groups are grains, fruits, vegetables, and protein. A healthy diet must have food from every group.

Do you eat food from every group? This chart can help you find out.

Five Food Groups

Dairy	Grains	Fruits	Vegetables	Protein
milk	bread	apples	lettuce	egg
cheese	rice	bananas	carrots	nuts
yogurt	pasta	oranges	broccoli	meat

What are two proteins?

Name one grain that you eat.

What dairy food do you eat most?

Make Connections

Which foods on the chart come from animals? Which foods come from plants? **Essential Question**

(tl) PhotoObjects.net/Getty Images; (tcl) IT Stock/PunchStock; (tc) I. Rozenbaum & F. Cirou/PhotoAlto; (tcr) I. Rozenbaum & F. Cirou/PhotoAlto; (tr) Isabelle Rozenbaum & Frederic Cirou/PhotoAlto/Getty Images; (cl) Comstock/Jupiter Images; (clc) Ildi Papp/YAY Micro/age fotostock; (c) Ingram Publishing/age fotostock; (crc) Comstock/Jupiter Images; (cr) I. Rozenbaum & F. Cirou/PhotoAlto; (bcl) Ingram Publishing/SuperStock; (bc) Stockbyte/Getty Images; (bcr) Mark Steinmetz/McGraw-Hill Education; (br) John A. Rizzo/Photodisc/Getty Images; (bl) ami mataraj/Shutterstock.com

Glossary

What is a Glossary? A glossary can help you find the meanings of words. The words are listed in alphabetical order. You can look up a word and read it in a sentence. Sometimes there is a picture to help you.

Sample Entry

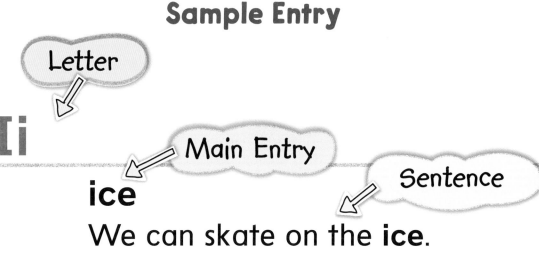

Letter

Ii

Main Entry

ice

We can skate on the **ice**.

Sentence

Bb

boy

The **boy** has red hair.

buy

We **buy** food at a store.

Cc

cow
This **cow** is black and white.

Ff

face
My **face** was just painted.

Gg

girl

The **girl** can jump rope.

green

The leaf is **green**.

Hh

happy

He smiles when he is **happy**.

home

Our **home** is very nice.

Ii

ice
We can skate on the **ice**.

Ll

lake
The **lake** looks blue.

line

Our class is in a **line**.

Oo

old

The car is very **old**.

Pp

plant

The **plant** is in dirt.

Ww

work

They **work** together.

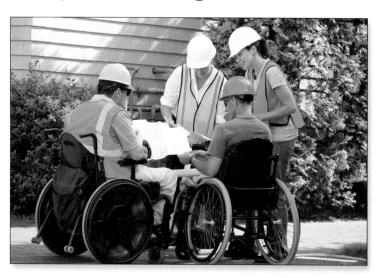

(t) M. Constantini/PhotoAlto, (b) Huntstock/The Agency Collection/Getty Images